Erin Pembrey Swan

Camels and Pigs

What They Have in Common

Franklin Watts - A Division of Grolier Publishing
New York • London • Hong Kong • Sydney • Danbury, Connecticut

For the Camels of Rajasthan

Photographs ©: Animals Animals: 6 bottom (Miriam Austerman), 19 (Robert Maier), 5 top right (Ralph A. Reinhold), 5 bottom left (Leonard Lee Rue III), 23 (Peter Weimann); NHPA: 25 (Martin Harvey), 36, 37 (Rich Kirchner), 33 (Stephen Krasemann), 15 (Eric Soder); Photo Researchers: 1 (James Balog), 5 bottom right (Mark N. Boulton/National Audubon Society), 5 top left (Kenneth W. Fink), 27 (Stephen J. Krasemann), cover (David Macias), 29 (Rod Planck), 13 (St. Meyers/Okapia); Superstock, Inc.: 40; Tony Stone Images: 35 (Jerry Alexander), 41 (Jack Daniels), 6 middle (Wayne Lastep), 7 (Penny Tweedie), 17, 21, 39, 42 (Art Wolfe); Visuals Unlimited: 31 (Joe McDonald), 6 top (William J. Weber).

Illustrations by Jose Gonzales and Steve Savage

Visit Franklin Watts on the Internet at:
http://publishing.grolier.com

Library of Congress Cataloging-in-Publication Data

Swan, Erin Pembrey.
Camels and pigs: what they have in common / Erin Pembrey Swan.
      p. cm. — (Animals in order)
   Includes bibliographical references and index.
   Summary: Describes members of the order of animals that have hooves with an even number of toes, including ibex, yaks, hippopotamus, deer, camels, and pigs.
   ISBN 0-531-11585-2 (lib. bdg.)   0-531-16400-4 (pbk.)
   1. Artiodactyls—Juvenile literature. [1. Ungulates.] I. Title. II. Series.
   QL737.U5S85 1999
   599.63—dc21   98-25108
                                                           CIP
                                                           AC

Contents

What is an Artiodactyl?

Have you ever seen animal footprints as you walked through a forest or along a riverbank? From squirrels to raccoons to bears, many animals leave their tracks behind in mud and snow.

On one of your walks through places where animals live, you might have noticed the tracks of a deer. Deer live in most North American forests. They have split hooves and leave tracks that look like two pointed toes. Deer tracks look very different from the paw prints left by raccoons or squirrels.

Deer are part of a special group, or *order*, of animals called *artiodactyls* (ahr-tee-oh-DAK-tuhls). Although many artiodactyls look a lot like deer, many others do not. Three of the four animals shown on the next page are artiodactyls. Can you guess which one is *not* an artiodactyl?

Yak

Horse

Mountain sheep

Hippopotamus

Traits of the Artiodactyls: Even-toed, Hoofed Animals

Deer hoof

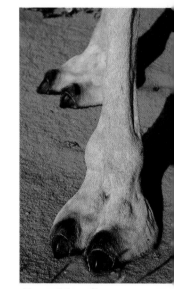

Camel hoof

Did you guess the horse? You were right! How can you tell a horse is not an artiodactyl? All artiodactyls have an even number of toes on each foot. The word artiodactyl means "even-toed." A horse's hoof has just one toe. Like deer, many artiodactyls have hooves split into two parts. Some artiodactyls, such as camels, have wide, two-toed feet that help the animals walk on soft ground like desert sand. The hippopotamus (hippo for short) is an artiodactyl with four toes on each foot.

Most artiodactyls eat plants. Their big, flat teeth are well suited for chewing grasses and leaves. Artiodactyls spend much of their time grazing and traveling from place to place to find food. Many kinds of artiodactyls live in *herds*, which makes them easy targets for meat-eating *predators*, such as lions and wolves. However, most artio-

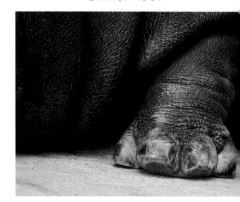

Hippo hoof

dactyls have springy hooves and strong legs that help them run fast to escape from enemies.

Artiodactyls are divided into two groups. The first group includes deer, goats, llamas, and giraffes. They eat only plants and have a special way of feeding. They chew their food briefly before swallowing it. Later, they "chew their *cud*." They bring food back up and chew it long and hard before swallowing it again. Animals that chew their cud are called *ruminants*. Many ruminants have horns or antlers that they use to defend themselves and their young from enemies.

A giraffe eating the branches of an acacia tree

The other group of artiodactyls includes pigs and hippos. They eat plants most of the time but sometimes use their long, sharp *canine teeth* to kill other animals for food. Artiodactyls in the second group do not chew their cud and do not have horns or antlers.

Wild artiodactyls are found in North America, South America, Europe, Africa, and Asia. They live in all sorts of places—forests, mountains, plains, and harsh deserts. No matter where you go, you have a chance to see an artiodactyl—or at least its tracks!

The Order of Living Things

A tiger has more in common with a house cat than with a daisy. A true bug is more like a butterfly than a jellyfish. Scientists arrange living things into groups based on how they look and how they act. A tiger and a house cat belong to the same group, but a daisy belongs to a different group.

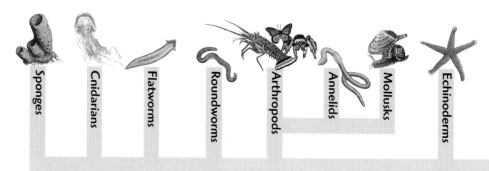

Sponges · Cnidarians · Flatworms · Roundworms · Arthropods · Annelids · Mollusks · Echinoderms

Animals

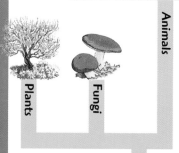

Plants · Fungi

Protists

Monerans

All living things can be placed in one of five groups called *kingdoms*: the plant kingdom, the animal kingdom, the fungus kingdom, the moneran kingdom, or the protist kingdom. You can probably name many of the creatures in the plant and animal kingdoms. The fungus kingdom includes mushrooms, yeasts, and molds. The moneran and protist kingdoms contain thousands of living things that are too small to see without a microscope.

8

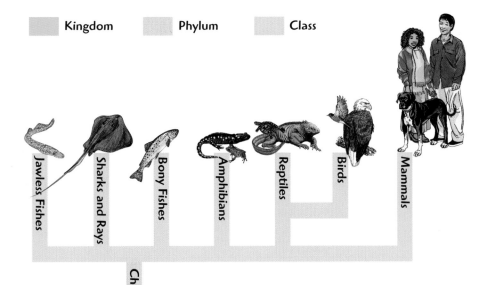

Kingdom   Phylum   Class

Jawless Fishes

Sharks and Rays

Bony Fishes

Amphibians

Reptiles

Birds

Mammals

Chordates

Because there are millions and millions of living things on Earth, some of the members of one kingdom may not seem all that similar. The animal kingdom includes creatures as different as tarantulas and trout, jellyfish and jaguars, salamanders and sparrows, elephants and earthworms.

To show that an elephant is more like a jaguar than an earthworm, scientists further separate the creatures in each kingdom into more specific groups. The animal kingdom can be divided into nine *phyla*. Humans belong to the chordate phylum. Almost all chordates have a backbone.

Each phylum can be subdivided into many *classes*. Humans, mice, and elephants all belong to the *mammal* class. Each class can be further divided into orders; orders into *families*, families into *genera*, and genera into *species*. All the members of a species are very similar.

How Artiodactyls Fit In

You can probably guess that artiodactyls belong to the animal kingdom. They have much more in common with bees and bats than with maple trees and morning glories.

Artiodactyls belong to the chordate phylum. Almost all chordates have a backbone and a skeleton. Can you think of other chordates? Examples include lions, mice, snakes, birds, fish, and whales.

The chordate phylum is divided into several classes. Artiodactyls belong to the mammal class. Mice, whales, dogs, cats, and humans are all mammals.

There are seventeen orders of mammals. Artiodactyls make up one of the four orders of mammals with hooves, which scientists call *ungulates*. Ungula is a Latin word that means "hoof, claw, or nail." Horses, rhinos, tapirs, and elephants are other kinds of ungulates. For millions of years, there were more odd-toed hoofed animals on Earth than any other kind of ungulate. However, over time, artiodactyls were more successful at finding food, and their numbers increased.

Today, there are ten families of artiodactyls. Each family is divided into a number of different genera and species. In this book, you will learn more about some of the artiodactyls.

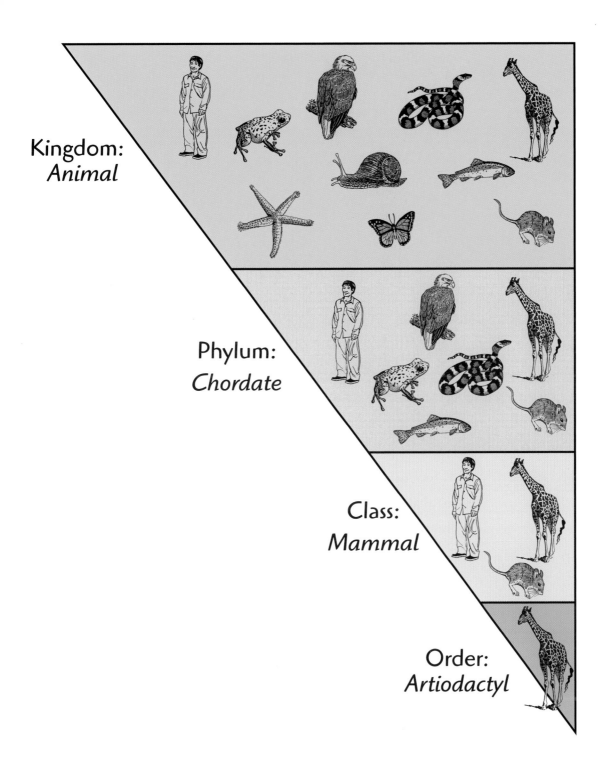

Kingdom:
Animal

Phylum:
Chordate

Class:
Mammal

Order:
Artiodactyl

Chamois

FAMILY: Bovidae
COMMON NAME: Chamois
GENUS AND SPECIES: *Rupicapra rupicapra*
SIZE: 30 inches (76 cm) high at the shoulder

Two young chamois (SHAM-ee) chase each other playfully across the rugged peaks of their mountain home. They skip easily from one rock ledge to another, never losing their footing on the steep European slopes. A tough pulplike tissue on their hooves helps them keep their balance on the rough ground.

Born in late spring, newborn chamois can stand almost at once. They follow their mothers as soon as they can walk. After only a few days, the youngsters can jump to amazing heights and climb easily along narrow rock ledges. Chamois are well suited for life in the high, snowy mountains.

Each female chamois, or *doe*, lives with her young in a herd of ten to thirty animals. In summer, they roam the slopes above the tree line, munching on grasses and flowers. When the winter snow starts falling, the chamois move below the tree line to feed on the shoots and dry leaves of woody plants. When they are not eating or roaming, chamois rest and chew their cud. Male chamois live alone most of the year but they join the females in the fall. The males fight to win mates, chasing one another over the slopes and jabbing their rivals with their sharp horns.

Every summer, a chamois grows a new set of rings on the lower part of its horns. You can tell a chamois's age by counting these rings.

Ibex

FAMILY: Bovidae
COMMON EXAMPLE: Alpine ibex
GENUS AND SPECIES: *Capra ibex*
SIZE: 26 to 41 inches (66 to 104 cm) high at
the shoulder

Two male ibex rise on their hind legs and crash their horns together. The animals keep pushing against each other until one of them backs down. The winner gets one of the females as his mate. These battles may look violent, but they rarely cause any real damage.

Alpine ibex, also called wild goats, live in the Alps—the highest mountain range in Europe. As they climb from rock to rock, the ibex grip the slopes with their split hooves. In summer, they may live as high as 10,000 feet (3,050 m) above sea level! When the heavy snows of winter come, the ibex move down the mountain. They prefer southern slopes where the sun warms the winter air. As they scramble across the rocks, ibex feed on the grasses and leaves of mountain shrubs. When spring comes, they nibble the new green shoots. When they aren't eating, ibex rest and chew their cud.

An ibex's horns never stop growing, and a new ridge appears every year. The horns of a male ibex may grow up to 5 feet (1.5 m) long!

Camels

FAMILY: Camelidae
EXAMPLE: Bactrian camel
GENUS AND SPECIES: *Camelus bactrianus*
SIZE: 6 feet (2 m) high at the shoulder

As the winter winds howl, a long line of bactrian camels make their way across an Asian desert. The camels close their lips and nostrils tightly against the blowing snow and sand. Fine hairs protect the insides of their ears. Bushy eyebrows and long, curly eyelashes keep their eyes safe.

Bactrian camels are well suited to life in the deserts of northern Asia, where winters are bitterly cold and summers are blazingly hot. Their thick, shaggy coats keep them warm even when the temperature is below zero. When summer comes, the animals shed their undercoats to keep cool.

Camels can survive in the harshest climates. Because they have tough mouths, they can eat the thorniest desert plants. They can also live for a long time without water or food. A bactrian camel uses its double humps to store fat. The camel's body changes the fat into nutrients when the animal can't find food or water. When the fat is all used up, the humps get flabby and flop sideways. When the camel eats, the humps firm up again.

Camels are sometimes called "ships of the desert" because Asian people use them to carry heavy loads across deserts. A camel's wide, tough feet help it travel easily across sand and rocky plains. Most camels are gentle with humans, but they can be dangerous if they feel threatened or annoyed. An angry camel will bite and kick, and may even spit or vomit in an attacker's face.

Yaks

FAMILY: Bovidae
COMMON NAME: Yak
GENUS AND SPECIES: *Bos grunniens*
SIZE: 5 to 6 feet (1.5 to 2 m) high at the shoulder

A herd of female yaks and their young roam the high mountains of Tibet in search of food. It is the middle of summer, and the yaks have climbed to the highest peaks, where the snow never melts. Yaks don't mind the cold, but they cannot survive hot weather for long.

Yaks are skilled at finding food in the snow. They paw the snow with their hooves or brush it aside with their broad muzzles. Then they nibble and tear at the tasty grasses underneath. If water is scarce, yaks eat snow to quench their thirst. When they're not grazing, the yaks rest and chew their cud.

Yaks are closely related to cattle, and the Tibetan people have tamed some of them. The yak's ability to survive the coldest weather makes it a good pack animal on the treeless plateaus of Asia. Its tough hooves help it travel over the roughest ground.

In late summer, wandering herds of males join the females to mate. The next spring, each female gives birth to one calf. The calf stays with its mother for at least a year. When the young yak is fully grown, its long hair almost reaches the ground. Adult male yaks weigh as much as 1,800 pounds (810 kg) and have horns up to 3 feet (1 m) long!

19

Hippopotamus

FAMILY: Hippopotamidae
COMMON NAME: Hippopotamus
GENUS AND SPECIES: *Hippopotamus amphibius*
SIZE: 5 feet (1.5 m) high at the shoulder

A hippopotamus walks gracefully along a riverbed, grazing on juicy water plants. After about 5 minutes underwater, the hippo returns to the surface to breathe. Because its eyes, ears, and nostrils are on the top of its head, the huge animal can keep most of its body underwater all day long. Hippos are the only artiodactyls that spend much of their time in water.

At sundown, the hippo lumbers out of the water and plods through the African jungle to its nighttime grazing grounds. Its thick skin oozes a reddish, oily liquid that keeps it moist when it isn't in water. In the past, people thought that hippos sweated blood!

The huge, bulky animals defend their *territories* fiercely against other hippos. Male hippos rush into these battles with their huge mouths wide open. They fight until one of them gives up and retreats. Sometimes the males try to drive their long, sharp tusks into each other's sides. A male hippo may have many scars from such fights.

The female hippo gives birth in the spring. She has a single calf that may weigh up to 100 pounds (45 kg). Mother hippos fiercely defend their babies against lions, crocodiles, and leopards. Plenty of hungry predators would love a taste of young hippopotamus!

Giraffes

FAMILY: Giraffidae
COMMON NAME: Giraffe
GENUS AND SPECIES: *Giraffa camelopardalis*
SIZE: 14 to 19 feet (4.5 to 6 m)

On a grassy plain in southern Africa, a giraffe nibbles at the top branches of an acacia tree. Its long tongue and flexible upper lip help the animal nibble on the acacia's juicy leaves and avoid the tree's many thorns. The giraffe's long legs and neck make it easy for the animal to graze on the tops of the tallest trees.

But long legs make it difficult for a giraffe to graze on the ground, and it isn't easy to drink from a watering hole either. To reach the water, a giraffe spreads its front legs far apart and bends its neck way down. This awkward position doesn't allow the animal to watch for lions and other predators.

The giraffe's unique, dark-spotted body blends in with the light and shadows in a grove of trees, helping to hide the animal from its enemies. If a giraffe is attacked, it may be able to escape. Even with its stiff-legged gait, a giraffe can run up to 35 miles (56 km) an hour. If the giraffe is forced to fight, it kicks its sharp, split hooves and swings its heavy neck back and forth to strike at its attacker.

Females give birth in the spring, standing up. The long-legged newborn drops more than 5 feet (1.5 m) to the ground! Just 10 hours later, the baby is running. Soon the young giraffe is able to roam the plains with its mother.

Wildebeests

FAMILY: Bovidae
COMMON EXAMPLE: Blue wildebeest
GENUS AND SPECIES: *Connochaetes taurinus*
SIZE: 45 to 55 inches (114 to 140 cm) high
at the shoulder

It is May on the Serengeti Plain in East Africa, the beginning of the dry season. More than a million blue wildebeests are traveling north. Along the way, zebras, gazelles, and other grazing animals join them. The herds are migrating to the open woodlands, where they can find leaves, twigs, grass, and water for the next 6 months. When the rainy season begins again, the wildebeests will return to the Serengeti to graze on the new lush grass and drink from the overflowing watering holes.

Most wildebeest calves are born during a 3-week period in the rainy season. The newborn calves can find safety in numbers. A prowling lion may have trouble separating one calf from such a large herd. Wildebeest cows roam with their calves in nursery herds, wandering from the territory of one wildebeest bull to another. Bulls guard their territories fiercely and fight one another to keep their cows. The bulls call the females with loud, deep grunts. If that fails, they chase the females and force them back to the herd.

The blue wildebeest, also called the brindled gnu, has a large head and long, curved horns. It has dark stripes on its head and

neck. It is the most common species of wildebeest on the African plain. Many black wildebeests once roamed the Serengeti, but most were killed off by human hunters. However, much of the Serengeti Plain is now a national park in the country of Tanzania. Animals inside the park are protected from hunters, and the number of black wildebeests is slowly increasing.

Deer

FAMILY: Cervidae
COMMON EXAMPLE: White-tailed deer
GENUS AND SPECIES: *Odocoileus virginiana*
SIZE: 4 feet (1 m) high at the shoulder

At dusk, a group of white-tailed deer gather at a small stream to drink. A *buck* watches over three does and their *fawns*. When they finish drinking, the deer wander back into the North American woods. They roam from one clearing to another, grazing on leaves and grasses. At sunrise, the deer rest on grassy beds and chew their cud.

In the winter, white-tailed deer often can't find enough food to eat. They gather in a grove of trees and trample deep snow into a flat *yard*. There they nibble bark and twigs while they wait for the snow to melt.

Only the bucks have antlers. In late fall, the males fight over the does. The forest echoes with the sounds of antlers crashing together. When mating season is over, the bucks shed their antlers. Mice, squirrels, and porcupines gnaw on the antlers to get minerals out of them. In spring, the bucks grow new antlers. At first, a fuzzy substance called *velvet* covers the antlers. Blood vessels in the velvet feed the antlers and help them grow. In late summer, the bucks rub against trees and bushes to remove the velvet and uncover the hard, sharp tips.

Deer have many enemies—from coyotes and mountain lions to humans. If danger threatens, the deer freeze briefly and then run away. As they run, they flick their white tails, warning other deer: "Watch out! Danger!"

Mountain Sheep

FAMILY: Bovidae
COMMON EXAMPLE: Rocky mountain
bighorn sheep
GENUS AND SPECIES: *Ovis canadensis*
SIZE: 42 inches (107 cm) high at the shoulder

In late fall, high in the Rocky Mountains, two male mountain sheep, or *rams*, face each other, growling and pawing the ground. They walk a short distance away from each other, turn back, rise on their hind legs, and charge. Crash! Their huge horns bang together. Sometimes these battles go on for hours, but they usually end after only four or five charges. When one ram turns away, he is admitting defeat. The other ram chooses a mate from among the female sheep, called *ewes*.

A bighorn ram's horns are an impressive sight. They don't fall off every year, as antlers do, but continue to grow throughout the ram's life. The horns may curve up to 4 feet (1.2 m) and weigh as much as 30 pounds (13.5 kg)—that's more than all the bones in the ram's body weigh! You can tell the age of a bighorn sheep by looking at its horns. If they form a complete circle, the sheep is very old.

During the summer, mountain sheep clamber among the highest peaks, munching on grasses, *lichens*, and seeds. In winter, the animals move to the lower slopes in search of food. In spring, they climb higher again. The ewes give birth on high rocky ledges where the lambs are safe from hungry mountain lions.

Muskox

FAMILY: Bovidae

COMMON NAME: Muskox

GENUS AND SPECIES: *Ovibos moschatus*

SIZE: 5 feet (1.5 m) high at the shoulder

A herd of muskox roams across the snowy Alaskan *tundra*. They paw through the snow, searching for grass to eat. The sharp rims and soft pads of their hooves keep them from slipping as they travel across rough ground. An undercoat of soft, woolly hair under their shaggy outer coat keeps the animals warm in bitter cold weather. When spring comes, they shed the undercoat.

Muskox live on cold northern plains of North America and Greenland. They eat any kind of plant, but grasses, willows, and Arctic flowers are their favorite foods. They travel in herds all year. Sometimes a female, or cow, leads the herd.

In August, bulls fight over the cows, crashing their big horns together. The winner's strong scent attracts a herd of cows. Young muskox are born in late May. When they are just a few hours old, they can stand and walk along behind their mothers, but they won't be fully grown for 5 or 6 years.

Muskox have a special way of driving off enemies. The herd forms a circle with their heads facing out and their horns lowered. The bulls take turns rushing at the enemy. Muskox are very fierce animals. They will fight any predator—wolf or human—to the death.

Peccaries

FAMILY: Tayassuidae
COMMON EXAMPLE: Collared peccary
GENUS AND SPECIES: *Tayassu tajacu*
SIZE: 22 inches (56 cm) high at the shoulder

Run! Danger! Bristles raised, a collared peccary barks loudly to warn others in the herd. The peccaries scurry away to hide in the underbrush and wait for the hungry jaguar to pass by. Peccaries are timid. They will run from enemies if they can. But, when necessary, peccaries defend themselves fiercely. They bite and slash with their long, razorlike teeth. Peccaries fighting as a group can drive off wild dogs and coyotes—and sometimes even a jaguar.

Collared peccaries are small, piglike animals that live in the woodlands and rain forests of Central and South America. They are usually noisy—snorting, grunting, and even barking as they fight over food. Unlike most artiodactyls, peccaries will eat almost anything. They feed on acorns, fruit, mushrooms, and grasses, as well as small animals. They can smell plant bulbs 6 inches (15 cm) under the soil! They dig the bulbs out with their snouts and gobble them up.

Collared peccaries are very social and travel in herds of up to fifty animals. A gland on the peccary's back gives off an oily substance, which it rubs onto trees and shrubs. The strong smell tells other peccaries where the animal has been. Peccaries know one another by smell and use scent to keep the herd together.

Llama

FAMILY: Camelidae
COMMON NAME: Llama
GENUS AND SPECIES: *Lama glama*
SIZE: 3 feet (1 m) high at the shoulder

A group of llamas winds down the mountain in a single file. They live in the Andes, a mountain range in South America. Tamed by the local people, the long-necked, woolly animals can travel up to 20 miles (32 km) a day, carrying loads that weigh up to 75 pounds (34 kg). If a load is too heavy, however, a llama may just lie down and refuse to move.

Although guanacos and vicuñas—their close relatives—roam wild, most llamas are *domestic animals*. Like their cousins the alpacas, the llamas have been tamed by humans. People use them not only as pack animals but also for wool, meat, and leather. Llama droppings are sometimes used as fuel.

Like most artiodactyls, llamas graze during the day. They feed on shrubs, lichen, and grasses. If a llama is angry, it may vomit in the face of its attacker, just like a camel. But llamas are usually so gentle that even children can ride on them.

A llama mates every 2 years, in July, and the female gives birth to one baby—or, once in a while, twins! The newborns have long, thin necks and legs but soon grow into sturdy adults with thick, fleecy coats.

Wild guanacos and vicuñas drive their 1-year-olds away to form separate herds, but human owners keep the tame young llamas within the herd. When the youngsters get older, their thick wool is woven into rugs and warm clothing.

Moose

FAMILY: Cervidae
COMMON NAME: Moose
GENUS AND SPECIES: *Alces alces*
SIZE: 7 feet (2 m) high at the shoulder

A bull moose stands chest-deep in a Canadian lake, nibbling at the tasty yellow water lilies floating on the surface. Every so often, he dips his head underwater and tears plants from the lake bottom with his strong teeth.

Moose can dive as deep as 18 feet (5.5 m), stay underwater for half a minute at a time, and swim for miles without stopping. Air fills the hollow hairs of their coats, helping them stay afloat. On land, moose browse on the leaves and twigs of trees and tall shrubs. They often raise their heads and look for enemies while they chew.

Like other deer, a bull moose sheds his antlers every winter. During mating season, he uses his wide, hard antlers to battle other bulls. The bulls clash head-on, pushing and shoving with their antlers until one gives up and goes away.

Bulls and cows meet only in late fall. This is when they mate. Cows call out with moaning cries, and bulls answer with hoarse grunts until they find one another. The rest of the year, they live apart. Where food is plentiful, bulls and cows may gather to feed in the same area, but they pay no attention to one another at all.

Caribou

FAMILY: Cervidae
COMMON NAME: Caribou
GENUS AND SPECIES: *Rangifer caribou*
SIZE: 4 feet (1.2 m) high at the shoulder

In early May, hundreds of caribou move north from the Alaskan tundra to their summer grazing grounds. The huge herd is made up of does, or females, and their newborn fawns. They will travel about 400 miles (640 km), using the same well-worn trails they have used for years. The bucks will follow a few weeks later. On the journey, the animals shed their winter coats, leaving clumps of matted hair caught in the shrubs and bushes along their route.

During the brief northern summer, caribou feed on grasses, lichens, and mosses. They grow strong and fat, ready to face the long winter. An adult caribou eats about 12 pounds (5.5 kg) of food each day!

Both male and female caribou have antlers. Bucks shed their antlers in early winter and begin growing them back in the spring. Does' antlers are smaller and thinner. They drop off in June and begin to grow back a few months later.

Caribou are well suited to cold weather. Their thick coats keep them warm, and their wide hooves act like snowshoes, helping the animals to walk in deep snow. They also use their scoop-shaped hooves to dig through the snow and find food. The grass underneath may be frozen, but it keeps them alive until spring.

Artiodactyls and People

Many centuries ago, people began to tame wild artiodactyls, such as pigs, goats, sheep, and cows. Those animals became the domestic farm animals we know today. People give artiodactyls food and shelter because they provide many things we use. Are you wearing a woolen sweater? The wool was sheared from a sheep or a llama, spun into yarn, and knitted into your sweater. Maybe you have a leather belt or leather shoes. Leather is made from the hides of cows.

Artiodactyls serve people in other ways too. From bacon to hamburgers, most of the meat people eat comes from artiodactyls. Cows, goats, and sheep give us milk, which also provides

This sheep's wool may be used to make wool sweaters, mittens, or hats

the main ingredient for cheese and ice cream. Camels carry heavy loads across the harsh deserts of Asia and the Middle East. In Tibet and Nepal, yaks work as pack animals and provide meat and milk.

Domestic animals are not the only artiodactyls that we use. People have always hunted wild animals for food and hides. White-tailed deer are the most common target of hunters in North America, and many African tribes still depend on wildebeests and gazelle herds for food.

Hunting and eating wild animals is often necessary for human survival, but people must be careful not to kill too many animals of one species. Millions of people throughout the world need food, and wild animals

Bacon, ham, and sausage are made from pig meat.

can't supply enough meat to feed everyone. Many species of artiodactyls have almost disappeared due to hunting.

Hunting isn't the only threat to artiodactyls. The number of human beings on Earth increases each year. More people need more land and cut down more trees for farming and building. In the

Giraffes live in many of Africa's national parks.

process, people destroy the natural homes of many animals and leave fewer places where wild animals can live.

However, people have begun to understand that they must protect animals. Governments all over the world have passed laws that make it illegal to hunt certain animals. For example, the number of muskox has grown since the Canadian government passed laws to protect them from hunters.

Some countries have also set aside land as national parks. These wilderness areas are protected by law, and the animals that live there cannot be hunted. Today, most wild artiodactyls, from giraffes to the last herds of bison, live in national parks around the world. However, despite efforts to save and protect wild artiodactyls, many of these animals are still in danger.

Words to Know

artiodactyl—a member of an order of hoofed mammals that have an even number of toes on each foot.

buck—a male of many species of deer, rabbits, kangaroos, and other animals. The female of these species is called a doe.

canine teeth—pointed teeth used for ripping or tearing.

class—a group of creatures within a phylum that share certain characteristics.

cud—a wad of swallowed plant matter that some artiodactyls bring up from the stomach to chew a second time.

doe—a female of many species of deer, rabbits, kangaroos, and other animals. The male of these species is called a buck.

domestic animal—a type of animal that has been tamed for use by humans.

ewe—a female sheep.

family—a group of creatures within an order that share certain characteristics.

fawn—a young deer.

genus (plural **genera**)—a group of creatures within a family that share certain characteristics.

herd—a group of animals that travel and eat together.

kingdom—the largest group of biological classification.

lichen—a mosslike growth found on trees and rocks. It consists of an alga and a fungus that live and grow together.

mammal—a warm-blooded animal that feeds its young with mother's milk and usually has some hair covering its skin.

order—creatures within a class that share certain characteristics.

phylum (plural **phyla**)—a group of creatures within a kingdom that share certain characteristics.

predator—an animal that hunts and eats other animals.

ram—a male sheep.

ruminant—an animal that chews its cud.

species—a group of creatures within a genus that share certain characteristics. Members of a species can mate and produce young.

territory—an area that is occupied and defended by an animal or group of animals.

tundra—a cold, dry region where trees cannot grow.

ungulate—a hoofed mammal.

velvet—the covering that nourishes a deer's antlers as they grow.

yard—a place in the woods where deer trample the snow flat so they can browse during the winter snows.

Learning More

Books

Alden, Peter. *Peterson First Guide to Mammals of North America.* Boston: Houghton Mifflin, 1987.

Fair, Jeff. *Moose for Kids.* Minocqua, WI: Northword Press, 1993.

Few, Roger. *MacMillan Animal Encyclopedia for Children.* New York: Simon & Schuster, 1991.

Landau, Elaine. *Desert Mammals.* Danbury, CT: Children's Press, 1997.

————. *Grassland Mammals.* Danbury, CT: Children's Press, 1997.

————. *Mountain Mammals.* Danbury, CT: Children's Press, 1997.

Wolpert, Tom. *Whitetails for Kids.* Minocqua, WI: Northword Press, 1991.

Web Site

Introduction to Artiodactyla
http://www.ipl.org/exhibit/dino/artiodactyls.html
Why do cows have a stomach with four compartments? Do all camels have two humps? To learn the answers to these questions and more, check out this site.

Index

About the Author

Erin Pembrey Swan studied animal behavior, literature, and early childhood education at Hampshire College in Massachusetts. She also studied literature and history at the University College of Galway in Ireland. Her poetry has been published in *The Poet's Gallery: The Subterraneans* and *The Poet's Gallery: Voices of Selene* in Woodstock, New York, and in *The Cuirt Journal* in Galway, Ireland. Ms. Swan is the author of two other books in the Animals in Order series. Although she lives in New Paltz, New York, Ms. Swan spends a great deal of time traveling to different parts of the world.